Zero-Sum Cost Marketplace:

The Future of Free Enterprise.

Ernst Hyacinthe

Library of Congress Control Number: 2013906209

ISBN:
978-0-9888098-0-2

DEDICATION

This book is dedicated to my family.

CONTENTS

	Acknowledgments	i
1	Introduction	1
2	THE ZERO-SUM COST MARKETPLACE: THE FUTURE OF FREE ENTERPRISE	3
3	HISTORY OF THE CENTRAL BANK FROM REVOLUTION TO WWI	7
4	THE GREAT DEPRESSION AND KEYNES VERSUS VON HAYEK	10
5	MORE RECENT HISTORY OF BOOMS AND BUSTS	16
6	JOHN NASH CONTRIBUTION	19
7	HERB SIMON AND BOUNDED RATIONALITY	21
8	ROBERT SOLOW INPUT	34
9	LOGISTICS AND SUPPLY CHAIN MANAGEMENT:THE ELEMENTS FOR A ZERO-SUM COST MARKET PLACE	36
10	FRAMING THE QUESTION	40

CONTENTS

11   DEFINITION / MOTIVATION FOR LOGISTICS   43

12   DEFINITION / MOTIVATION FOR SUPPLY   51
     CHAIN MANAGEMENT

13   DEFINITION / MOTIVATION FOR A ZERO-   59
     SUM COST® MARKET PLACE

14   HOW TO ACHIEVE A ZERO-SUM COST®   64
     MARKET PLACE

15   RELATIONSHIP BETWEEN LOGISTICS,   66
     SUPPLY CHAIN MANAGEMENT AND THE
     ZERO-SUM COST® MARKET PLACE

16   THE SUCCESSES OF LOGISTICS AND SUPPLY   68
     CHAIN MANAGEMENT CREATE THE
     ENVIRONMENT FOR A DYNAMIC AND
     SUSTAINABLE ZERO-SUM COST® MARKET
     PLACE

17   HOW CAN BUSINESS EVOLVE IN THIS   76
     PARADIGM

18   SOME INDUSTRIES WHICH COULD   87
     INCORPORATE ZSC SEAMLESSLY

19   CONCLUSION   90

     REFERENCES   95

     INDEX   100

ACKNOWLEDGMENTS

Mat 9: 37-38

1 INTRODUCTION

The zero-sum cost marketplace proposes to bring consumers into the supply chain as equity partners in order to, eventually, reduce consumer costs to zero. The method is built on a strong foundation of both Keynesian and monetarist economic policies, combined with the inevitably technologically advanced Internet marketplace. The zero-sum cost marketplace is similar to, but is in addition to, the loyalty bonus structure of many big retailers. With this method, some percentage of the gross sale to the customer is placed in a trust investment account. Over time, with compounding interest or appreciation, these contributions increase in value to cover the original transaction cost.

By inclusion in the "cradle to grave" product life cycle, the consumer provides valuable feedback to the supply-chain stakeholders. Suppliers, from raw materials to wholesalers, mine information regarding consumer appetite for goods and services as well as consumer concerns over social and ethical issues, corporate governance, corporate citizenship, and environmental compliance. Consumers are evolving into a more activist group. Successful businesses will respond to these concerns. The value added is lower-cost supply chains, greater customer loyalty, and a less volatile financial market. The investment aspect creates capital to modernize technology and, by extension, smooths out economic fluctuations that create "boom and bust" cycles. With the universe of potential goods and services the Internet provides, suppliers need to combat commoditizing with personality, also known as branding. Brands need to conform to the modern consumer's desire for more self-actualization than pure survival. Wealth and investments factor in esteem and actualization—what could be more personal to the consumer?

2 THE ZERO-SUM COST MARKETPLACE: THE FUTURE OF FREE ENTERPRISE

"Over the long term, places with strong, distinctive identities are more likely to prosper than places without them. Every place must identify its strongest, most distinctive features and develop them or run the risk of being all things to all persons and nothing special to any...Livability is not a middle-class luxury. It is an economic imperative."

—Robert Solow

Economic Nobel Laureate Robert Solow developed a growth model distinguishing the values of different "vintages" of capital. Old capital backs old technology by its nature, while the profits derived from old technology, if reinvested, tend toward investing in newer technology. Since Solow calculated about 80 percent of the growth in the United States to be driven by technological progress, investment in new technology becomes critical to the nation's growth path. Consistent and continuous investment smooths out the business cycles.

Zero-sum cost market provides a growing pool of ready capital drawn from favored consumer goods and services to be invested by end users ready to communicate their needs and desires through the supply chain. Although not intended to be a government initiative, it is very democratic in its function. Consumers vote with their money to govern the supply chain and, as a result, regulate commerce in an efficient manner that no government can match. The natural occurrence is businesses supplying consumers with preselected goods and services, using modern investment capital.

The computer age has allowed money markets and financial markets to flourish with direct and immediate access by small investors and consumers. New capital comes to money markets quickly. Money markets involve M2 money—liquid investments within a year of maturity. Financial markets involve longer-term investments. Stocks by their nature are financial instruments, since they do not expire. In other words, the individual small investor has been fully integrated into the asset allocation function of the economy, both in long-

and short-term markets. They save and invest online. With new technologies, new management techniques and devices, investors either maximize the profit, share costs more efficiently, or speed the transactions. A zero-sum cost marketplace accomplishes these goals.

Part of this evolution, however, is a change in consumerism. Traditionally, consumers bought off a shelf from a local merchant. In many ways, the local merchant provided the universe of possibilities, from which the consumer decided what best fit his needs. The merchant looks to supply profitable items. His wholesaler offers only a limited selection as well. Just like the merchant, the wholesaler attempts to maximize profit. The manufacturer tries to reduce costs along the assembly line. Reducing costs almost always reduces choices. The company supplying raw materials wants to make more money. Some are willing to cut some good citizenship corners to do so.

At each of these steps, the consumer has been left out of the discussion. Yet, consumer input may be the key to these decisions. If consumers define tolerance in terms of changing demand, it is good business to allow their feedback early in the system. Traditional marketing studias focus on product demands, not process demands toward the social meaning of the product. Between marketing research and the inevitable consumer Internet news cycle, dramatic changes in demand can occur.

The modern consumer has access to most of this process through Internet research vehicles. The basic tools exist to require every stakeholder to act under a certain code of ethics. Of course, the code needs to be negotiated. Consumers can demand a green ethic, an employee-appreciation ethic, a community-service ethic. Corporate brands will be established in this way: Internet consumerism.

The computer age has matured consumers. Consumers want to be involved in the major policy decisions of companies. Consumers view costs differently. This fact is best demonstrated by environmental compliance regulations. Free riders are no longer welcome. Everyone must clean up their own mess. Noncompliance is viewed as a cost shared by the community at large, rather than rightfully paid by the company.

The future of the zero-sum cost marketplace begins with lessons from the past. With this in mind, the following sections present a historical perspective.

3 HISTORY OF THE CENTRAL BANK FROM REVOLUTION TO WWI

Since the country's founding, the federal government of the United States has struggled with the role and control of a central bank. Tom Payne, Thomas Jefferson, and James Madison argued for state-chartered private banks only to issue bank notes as currency. Federal governments, in their view, could pay bills by simply printing money, and they would do so. Currency would devalue if not based on private credit practices and discipline. Stocks and bonds should trade on the reputation and financial strength of the issuers, not the regulation or guarantee of ever-changing personnel with differing agendas in the federal government. These three patriots took the monetarist view of the economy.

Alexander Hamilton viewed a central bank as a tool to smooth economic cycles. As a lender of last resort, the central bank could loan money from the reserves of all banks to the specific markets in need. In this way, all banks remain solvent, and the economy avoids the boom-bust cycle. Federal oversight or regulation of financial markets was not, at that time, a consideration. In 1791, Hamilton convinced George Washington to create a central bank to regulate all financial institutions.

Madison became president in 1811 and did not renew the charter of Hamilton's central bank. The end of the Civil War gave birth to the next central bank. It, too, lasted about twenty years.

In 1894, Friedrich Engels opined that the inventions of steamships, telegraphs, railroads, and the Suez Canal had shrunk the world enough to end all market collapses. Excess capital would spread quickly throughout the world, smoothing volatility issues, and local overspeculation would diminish to irrelevance (Mayer 2001, 1). Today, the Federal Reserve closely regulates financial institutions, banks, and the money supply. With the Internet world full of computers, day trading and financial markets became easily and universally available around the clock and around the world. In this day and age, Engels might have wrongly predicted the end of market collapses again.

In the wake of World War I, the Federal Reserve Act of 1913 formed a central bank with twelve regional banks. This compromised bank was not authorized to regulate disputes among the banks or with Washington, DC (Wells 2004). With the gold standard in place, the twelve banks could only print as much money as was reserved in gold. Milton Friedman said, "The 1974 removal of the prohibition against private ownership of gold in the United States was, somewhat paradoxically, a tribute to the end of gold's monetary role" (Friedman 1994, 250). The United States, and by extension, most of the rest of the world, became a fiat economy, one in which bank notes act as unsecured loans to the government. Since 1974, each decade has seen a major industry bust: oil in the 1970s, commercial real estate in the 1980s, technology stocks (dot-coms) in the 1990s, and residential real estate in 2000s. These are the talismans of the boom-bust cycles that were predicted by monetarist theorists if government had no checks on the amount of money it could print.

The combined nightmares of Jefferson, Madison, and Payne had become reality.

4 THE GREAT DEPRESSION AND KEYNES VERSUS VON HAYEK

John Maynard Keynes gave further voice to the Hamiltonian argument. Keynes challenged economic orthodoxy by championing government spending without limitation until the Great Depression -era unemployment problem subsided. The British suffered worse unemployment than the Americans during this era. Friedrich von Hayek was a young gun for the monetarist policy wonks specifically chosen to challenge Keynes. Von Hayek viewed unrestrained, underfinanced government spending—especially if financed through an expansion of the money supply—as a vehicle that would recklessly move the economy to perhaps a period of boom, but without a doubt, eventually toward another bust. Monetarists believe the illusion is the boom; the reality is the bust. Booms are misallocated resources, while busts are the result. Keynesian economics reflect a more liberal stance: if people are not economically surviving now, the boom-and-bust cycle will not matter. Economic planning is more humanitarian in nature, and therefore, central planning is justifiable.

The Great Depression featured massive unemployment, lost fortunes, and devastating poverty across the globe. The Keynes and von Hayek debate in England highlighted two distinct plans to recover from this bust period.

Maynard Keynes was a Cambridge professor who rewrote widely accepted economic theory to demonstrate how government fiscal policies could speed recovery. His basic philosophy involved unfinanced, unfunded spending by government until the depression ended. Summarized: government cannot cut its way out of a slump; it must grow itself out.

Monetarists, like von Hayek from the London School of Economics, wanted government spending maintained, but not expanded. They maintained that the natural forces of the market would stoke the engines. Slumps were, by their natures, times when poor investments were liquidated, a "pain-induced prudence," as Andrew Mellon said. Summarized: government spending and the consequential misallocation of assets caused the problem; more of the same is a toxic prescription.

Keynes theory is widely misunderstood, because

Keynes himself made the unfortunate statement that government, for lack of anything else better to do, could hire labor to dig holes and hire different labor to fill them, as long as employment rose. The context of the statement was that government should seek public improvement projects, schools, maintenance on holdings, innovation, or anything that might not ordinarily be accomplished through the free market system, but some public value existed for the completion of the task, and labor inputs were not being fully utilized. If all of those projects had been funded and "underemployment equilibrium" had not been reached, then the government should continue funding nonproductive employment.

Hayekians respond with historical data, which shows that an overspending government, or a government subsidizing one sector, creates a false boom in that sector of the economy, misallocates assets to that sector, and creates a new boom-bust cycle. The boom is false; the bust is the real result.

Keynesians counterargue the government will ultimately borrow from its subjects (or, in the US, citizens) and repay them with interest or an improved overall lifestyle. The government will spend money to help feed the unemployed; businesses and capitalists will not. The Keynesian philosophy of economics has an element of welfare—or, more correctly, "workfare." Keynes always pointed out that people became more enamored with his theories during downturns;

there are no monetarists in a depression.

Hayekians point out that double recessions and prolonged depressions would not occur were it not for extreme government interventions. When the government forces bad investments, like substandard mortgages, or launches premature solar energy companies, it actually depresses the economy more, because those assets are misallocated to wasteful entrepreneurship. Business cycles, or "fluctuations" as von Hayek called them, were natural and unstoppable and uncontrollable. The boom-bust cycle was government-induced and severely damaging.

Interestingly, the current government stimulus has had opposite-than-predicted effects. Keynesian models predicted a 9-percent unemployment peak without the stimulus package and 8 percent with the stimulus. The peak occurred at 10 percent with the stimulus package. The model predicted the correct difference, but the wrong direction. These results suggest a balance-sheet depression. Individuals and companies are paying off debt, and the money is being hoarded by lenders. In fact, and rather ironically, banks are being subsidized to the point that lending is foolish. Banks are being paid not to lend. Entrepreneurship has been dampened, so unemployment has remained relatively high. Stakeholders have been stimulated to shed bad debt and poor investments. The end result: the investor's moral hazard is being reduced. Interestingly, consumers are paying down credit-card and other short-term debt, but long-term debt is increasing proportionately. Pain-induced prudence seems to rule again.

The zero-sum cost market strategy buffers these busts by not misallocating assets from the beginning. Consumer/investors ultimately rule asset allocation mechanisms to manipulate the right quantity of supplies to meet their admitted demand. Secondly, the consumer can reallocate capital during a bust to avoid deeper recessions and depressions. Government expenditures and market manipulation never works efficiently— review the collapse of the Soviet Union, for example. Consumer-driven investment is efficient, and in the zero-sum cost scenario, available without creating massive debt.

"All production is for the purpose of ultimately satisfying a consumer. Time usually elapses, however—and sometimes much time—between the incurring of costs by the producer (with the consumer in view) and the purchase of the output by the ultimate consumer. Meanwhile the entrepreneur (including both the producer and the investor in this description) has to form the best expectations he can as to what the consumers will be prepared to pay when he is ready to supply them (directly or indirectly) after the lapse of what may be a lengthy period; and he has no choice but to be guided by these expectations, if he is to produce at all by processes which occupy time" (Keynes 1964, 46).

How can consumers and the business sector partner in a free market economy to assure investment, savings, spending, employment, income, and production all continue at sustainable growth rates?

Other economists and thinkers have suggested solutions, building on the Keynes versus von Hayek debates. The zero-sum cost market strategy combines the Keynesian "top down" view with the monetarist "bottom up" view. In fact, the zero-sum cost market strategy creates a circular motion to the "cash to cash" cycle.

5 MORE RECENT HISTORY OF BOOMS AND BUSTS

The Federal Reserve's (Fed) definition of M1 money includes cash not in the Fed—that is, in circulation—plus demand deposits, such as checking accounts. The Fed prints money to control the supply of currency, both in the sense of replacing worn-out currency and expanding (or more rarely, contracting) M1. Since M1 includes demand deposits, the velocity of trades—that is, the number of times the same currency is transferred in a given timeframe—may affect the amount kept in checking accounts. Thrift and investment affect M1 as well, as moving cash from consumerism to investment decreases M1. For example, in 1991, the money supply rose 12.6 percent—at that time, a record. Transactions were not occurring rapidly, because people were not buying consumer goods—they were investing, saving, and repaying short-term debt. Subtly, this investment boom implies that basic survival needs were being met. The middle class was no longer concerned with minimum standards; luxury was the new target of acquisition. Finally, investors bought stock in technology and communications, causing a stock market rise: asset inflation instead of consumer inflation. The ensuing "wealth" dividend sparked the consumer side of the market. The technology bubble burst soon thereafter (Mayer 2001, 220).

The savings and loan crisis in the late 1980s and early 1990s lead to that recession. Black (2005, 9) indicates the S&L industry in the 1990s was insolvent by about $150 billion due to rampant fraud and overspeculation in investment strategies. An announced increase in capital gains taxes on real estate investments caused something of a selling panic in an oversupplied market. The Federal Savings and Loan Insurance Corporation (FSLIC) had about $6 billion in funds to cover the $150 billion shortfall in liquidity. FSLIC was itself insolvent. The S&L managers were able to reap big rewards for speculation, and the downside was covered by FSLIC insurance—in other words, the customers would not sue for fraud because they suffered no damages, and nobody in government wanted this known, because this intervention created a moral and economic hazard. So banks, with well-funded Federal Deposit Insurance

Corporation (FDIC)insurance, were encouraged to buy savings and loans, and the stronger savings and loans became savings banks. The money pumped into the economy did not expand the money supply; it simply exchanged assets. The development industry, though, was in one of the biggest busts in fifty years.

The money supply is affected by the actual supply of currency, consumer transactions, consumer price inflation, and the competition between consumer demand and investment demand, or thrift. The other factor is crisis. Fixing the economy usually involves exchanging or revaluing assets rather than increasing production until the wealth equilibrium is reestablished.

The pattern in these boom-and-bust cycles is the desire to resolve a social issue, which in turn creates the demand to change the rules in some way. The business equilibrium readjusts, causing some pain.

In the zero-sum cost marketplace, these cycles diminish in size and regularity, because the consumers are in charge of supply-side decisions directly. Plus, in the event of a recession, consumers have their savings to help with any income shortfalls without waiting for a government relief program.

6 JOHN NASH CONTRIBUTION

Some critics think that Nash attempted to modify Adam Smith's market theory by replacing the "invisible hand" or the self-regulating behavior of the market with a zero-sum game strategy that suggested individuals and groups succeed marginally better when the individual observes the actions of other participants and reacts to those forces. For example, Burger King competes with McDonald's by encouraging special orders rather than offering assembly-line burgers. Other critics see his contribution as an eloquent Mathematical proof with extensive implications for theoretical economics.

The zero-sum game strategy implies two conditions. Individuals in a group seek feedback and create strategies based on other members' actions, so the group maximizes utility in a competitive bidding market, even though each individual may not receive his original optimal choice. Subtly, this phenomenon suggests individuals begin in a group in order to conform, but differentiation becomes an economic good when individuals observe other members. Adam Smith's invisible hand is guided by group dynamics.

A preliminary interpretation of Nash's paper "Equilibrium Points in n-Person Games" suggests a convex figure like a hexagon or a circle will result in the mapping of the participants' decision matrix. It's a clear indication of a game strategy involving zero-sum cost, even though the Nash focus considered profit or classic utility to be the motivating factors in selecting a strategy.

A more comprehensive, multidisciplinary view, which is detailed in the next sections, completed Nash's thoughts.

7 HERB SIMON AND BOUNDED RATIONALITY

Herb Simon observed human behavior with a multidisciplinary approach born from his managerial past and social science academic career. Simon determined that traditional economists on both sides of the monetary/fiscal debate concerned themselves with what decisions were made rather than how decisions were made. (Hunt, 1980, 1)

Simon rejected classic economics' assumption that perfect knowledge existed prior to any decision based on his managerial observations. Interestingly, Simon made these observations as a young clerk in a public, that is government, office; the same background as Keynes. Simon derived the theory of bounded rationality in decision making.

(Simon, etal, 1987) Bounded rationality refers to choosing among known solutions with known data, or deciding to create a new solution (innovation) based on the belief that substantial improvement can be accomplished. Other factors, such as environmental ethics or improved lifestyle, were unquantifiable , un-measurable, and filled with uncertainty. So, although these considerations may be high priority, they cannot be part of a truly quantitative analysis.

Bounded rationality "refers to peoples limited ability to make comparisons, to see into the future, and, more generally, to process information". (Cyret, 1979, 63) Simon coined the term *satisficing* to indicate the optimal possible decision with which to achieve the perceived best outcome with imperfect information.

Simon observed and concluded human rationality to be bounded externally by social constraints and internally by cognitive restraints (Sent, 2005, 227). Truly free decisions depend upon non-conformity and unlimited possibility; but both are actually unquantifiable constraints in the process.

Bounded rationality is a decision making and problem solving theory not meant to strengthen neoclassical economic thought. Nash's game theory used utility and profit as a basis for decisions. Individual members of groups can not quantify the other members utility or economic profit; they can only guess. In Simon's theory, quantification enhances rationality; it does not help create it; or perhaps, it rationalizes the emotional decision to act. Management demands set the conditions for rational thought; therefore, some actions are predisposed to be nonworking solutions (Mankelwicz, 2010, 60). Common sense, or heuristics, applies available metrics as a screening tool. "Human perception may be as bounded in scope as our rationality". (Mankelwicz, 2010, 63). In an industrial psychological way, quantitative results may be viewed as symbols or talisman. Managers experience numbers as guideposts (Mankelwicz, 2010, 64) Different but related stakeholders, like the technical rationality people, quantification limiters, economic trenders, socially conscious, and political class, although largely invisible to a specific decision, impact all final decisions, and at a minimum, restrict the array of reasonable solutions, and therefore, possible outcomes. (Mankelwicz, 2010, 65).

Achieving perfect information defies logic and reason; it is not a rational basis for a decision making process. The managed decision making process is more akin to the scientific methods of laboratory testing and field data collection. Neither is the sole path to truth nor the sole source of perfect decisions. (Hunt, 1980, 2) Managers reach decisions through satisficing, but even more important, with the goal of achieving at least as optimal a decision as the competition. And, the

Ernst Hyacinthe

cost of optimization can be greater than the reward. (Hunt, 1980, 2) Satisficing relies on the available budget, specifically, costs.

The time variable causes poor allocation choices. Perfect knowledge scenarios imply divining the future demands of consumers or the supply side capacity to innovate. Neither side can predict the other; so this becomes less likely as the two sides drift apart during communications. When both sides communicate in the same supply chain, fewer errors are likely. Zero-Sum Cost mechanisms assure the consumer is literally invested in the supply side and has valuable input during the manufacturing or supply process. The supply and demand sides acknowledge the symbiotic relationship between them.

Nash focused on profit and utility optimization, Simon viewed cost and satisficing as more reflective of real world circumstances.

"A system may be defined as an orderly grouping of separate but interdependent components for the purpose of attaining some predetermined objective". (Mockler, 1968, 53) 1960's systems science creates a unifying theory of explanation regarding the interplay among differing expertise. Hierarchy, orderly arrangement of components, matters regardless of system or decision complexity. Interdependence relies upon communications. The system unifies through goal orientation. The system defines the decision making environment. (Mockler, 1968, 54) Ironically, the system also defines the possibilities from which a decision is made. For example, choosing a target outcome limits potential innovation. Think of a system as a project. The project begins with a goal. Just setting that goal can retard innovation. Project outcomes must be defined very broadly to allow the maximum number of considered solutions.

Bounded rationality rejects the long-established maximization theory. (Hutchuel, 2001, 260) Simon proposed design theory: creative thinking formulates the problem first. Problems are unfamiliar and poorly defined situations. His model to explain design theory involved two different decisions: either choose from solutions or goods that already exists or innovation, create something unique. *Regardless of which method is chosen, the success of the problem solver/decision maker rests in the hands of the consumer/end user.* Choosing existing solutions accepts conventional thoughts and mores. The reaction of the intended audience determines the successful creation of something. The irony of decision theory is that problem solving and decision making are skills which require practice, not a higher level of problem solving or decision making. (Hutchuel, 2001, 269)

The traditional quantitative unit of measurement for the soundness of decisions is Subjective Expected Utility (SEU). SEU quantitative analysis is not based on statistically driven decisions, but instead, perfect-knowledge decisions. For this reason, SEU theory translates poorly into real management applications, for example, the prisoners' dilemma, where each prisoner pursuing his own self-interest leads both prisoners to be worse off than had they not pursued their own self-interests. (Simon etal., 1987, 12) In actual laboratory testing in game theories, people satisfice, then react as mirror images to the other players. (Simon etal., 1987, 19) Problem framing affects the decision making process. SEU ignores examples such as: the credit card industry deciding whether price differences reflecting cash or card use should be referred to as (cash) discounts or (credit) surcharges. Even though the application has equivalent real effects, the psychology concerns legitimacy. Which is the normal condition, credit card purchases or paying cash? Conformity is a dear commodity. (Simon etal., 1987, 22)

As wealth increases, people become more averse to risk, and therefore, SEU results skew as wealth and status change. (Baskharan, etal, 2008, 233) Does this wealth bias reflect decision theory satisficing? The wealthy are more satisfied with their current condition, so any risk must pay higher dividends. The rich desire to get richer, or maintain their status quo.

Simon's career began with local government where the decisions making process intrigued him. He observed the process: how inputs were determined and the management reaction regarding the inputs. As a manifestation of human behavior in management, Simon breaks down administrative decision making into two major components:

1. **Cost Element:** project budget requirements for decision-making includes resourcing implementation of money, time and labor during the preparation phase through the compilation of data and information, classification, propose alternatives and evaluation phases.

2. **Resolution and aftermath:** This complex element relates to the goals defined by the decision maker, and how the problem is framed. Whether these goals conflict with personal, public service or for-profit public service goals. The extent to which the resolution harmonizes with the policy and the outlined desires of the organization.

Simon explains that the administrative decision cannot be rational 100%; so the public policy administrator must choose among available alternatives and solutions. Simon's thesis suggests the Director remains satisfied with solutions acceptable rather than optimal.

"A frequent practice in the social sciences is to bemoan our present ignorance while making optimistic predictions about future knowledge." (Simon 2001) Just before his death, Simon authored a summary article concerning the state-of-the-art decision making field of study. In that article (Simon 2001) Simon discussed the following:

1. **Operational Research and Management Science** (31-2). New mathematical tools available to managers being applied to decide good and best decisions. For profit companies utilize these tools more so than the public sector even though these tools have their genesis in World War II as operational analysis. The civilian government clings to the traditional economic models in their decision matrix.

2. **Optimality** (32-3): Scheduling procedures, such as Gantt Charts or *Program Analysis and Review Technique* (NetMBA 2011) (PERT) combining heuristic inputs and mathematical logic. Gaming scenarios and rigorous axiomatic systems advance management preparedness to make decisions or define problems.

3. **Experiments on Decision Making** (33-4): This area blossomed over the last few years of Simon's life. Organizational behavior and institutional group-think researched and studied processes within similar entities because real scenarios are hard to duplicate in the lab.

4. **Persuasion and Evocation** (34-5): The system processes premises or assumptions

(inputs), and draws conclusions (outputs). But the output, or conclusion, serves as the next input, or educated assumption. The persuasion cycle responds only to the selected premises, therefore, the assumption or premise shape the potential solutions or output. Unfortunately, conflicting inputs are not rare. This research questions the motivation of individuals or special interest groups to participate in inputs. The inputs steer a decision toward a desired goal, a corporate goal, or in the belief that the goal is in the best interest of the community. Ideology and self-interest are secondary hurdles compared to institutional structures that block communications, even in the case of foreign trade.

5. **The Structure of Decisions** (35-7): Systemized common sense refers to behavior and choice within an organization especially where conformity is a defining input. Computerization is a tool of this conformity.

Several studies have continued since Simon's death:

Quality in Innovation (Gidel etal, 2005)

- The choice to be innovative necessarily creates a new process by which to develop and implement the innovation (1). *This means that before a product can be designed, a project must be designed* (2).

- The risk management approach reflects traditional decision making and closely match the innovation processes with two exceptions (2):

  - Premature project design can decrease innovation.

  - Operational risk identification may damper innovation since the risks are either difficult to identify or impossible to estimate.

- The circumstances described cause a shift from performance management to value management, allowing local custom to have inputs (3) This leads to managing decisions for effectiveness rather than control of performance.

- Once a project is okayed by upper management, the project manager chooses a definition of success and models goals accordingly. Then the construction of the method begins.

- Five approaches to project construction are (5-6):

- Philosophical Approach: flexible to adapt to situations encountered, but not anticipated. It is a more iterative approach to risk management and project management where new knowledge is reconsidered in the overall meaning of project goals.

- Theoretical contributions and the quality principle: a more traditional optimization approach whereby all stakeholders are perfectly in tune with project goals.

  o Systemic modeling of the design process: helps in small bites of projects. It helps communications within a phase of a project but tends to become unclear in the big picture. Operationally, it helps facilitate design processes and redesign processes. But the two phases must be separated for efficiency.

- Experimentation
- Study and Comparison with other models

Benchmarking the project to control completion and scheduling keeps the stakeholders on the optimum path to completion.

Project management requires several specialty skills:

1. Objectification is the process of building a shared language and therefore purpose of project goals. Control the language, control the expertise and coordination.

2. Construction of Finalities relates to value

management. The final goal best achieves a value rather than a specific end.

3. Confrontation management referees the differing points of view which inevitably occur on projects. The feedback cycle reveals differences of opinion. The ultimate goal, though, must remain intact. Confrontation manages these differences and keeps the team participating fully.

4. Association of finality relates to everyone understanding how their task fits the big goals of the project. The interdependencies of the tasks. Communications are critical.

5. Anticipation refers to the need to understand and expect that intermediate goals change with new information. Anticipating these changes and embracing them as an acknowledgement that the objective has not been altered but the route to achieve it has. Knowledge of these conditions is important to all stakeholders.

The outlined method requires the proper company ethic of collaboration and understanding that projects continue under uncertain conditions, changing conditions.

This methodology builds on Simon's bounded rationality theory. However, others disagree and consider Simon to ignore context of decisions. (Mousavi and Garrison 2003) The basis for the disagreement is whether or not deliberation, part of the decision process, is end goal oriented or option gathering oriented. The context might be self-concern for keeping a job or being part of a group rather than an optimizing company decision (150).

If the individual redirects the thinking or deliberation of a project to fit personal satisficing, would an end user/consumer act in a similar manner? Isn't the consumer the target of the innovation or marketing question? When should the end user become part of the innovation team? The Zero-Sum Cost strategy does not require synchronized project starts and finishes. In fact, the elegance of the system implies if consumers are dissatisfied with a suppliers supply chain, they can simply seek a new supplier who will listen to the consumer. This process occurs before the product reaches the market, saving time and money for all parties to the transaction. Poor suppliers cut losses early. Unhappy consumers get appreciated products earlier. Market equilibrium is better served through the Zero-Sum Cost system.

8 ROBERT SOLOW INPUT

"If it is very easy to substitute other factors for natural resources, then there is, in principle, no problem. The world can, in effect, get along without natural resources." - Robert Solow

Of course, this comment was meant as a tongue in cheek rebuke to those economists ignoring dwindling resources as an element of future cost. Recycling technology reduces the need for virgin raw materials, but raw materials are still an important input. Managing the supply chain is important management technology.

Time may be considered an unbounded resource. The compounding of incomes plays a vital role in the Zero-Sum Cost marketplace. This strategy uses time to achieve a dynamic equilibrium and maintain a steady market. The unbounded but consistent nature of time characterizes investments which create a dynamic equilibrium.

Robert Solow coined the phrase, "measurement of our ignorance" to signify the 3% of his production model that was inexplicable by the model. Managerial efficiency may explain how, over time, business runs leaner, labor becomes more productive, or new technology is applied. Or, perhaps, bringing the end user into the mix earlier in the supply chain system would increase efficiency optimally.

9 LOGISTICS AND SUPPLY CHAIN MANAGEMENT:
THE ELEMENTS FOR A ZERO-SUM COST MARKET PLACE

Prior to the industrial revolution, the fundamental motivation behind almost all human activities was self-preservation, and since the internet revolution, the most important motivation might be self-promotion.

Neo-Malthusian theory builds on the works and philosophies of Thomas Malthus. Malthus' cynical theory regarded mankind as unsophisticated, and apt to reproduce until everyone lived on a subsistence level, and then population growth would be naturally slowed until the next technology supported a greater population. Neo-Malthusians view this theory as incomplete. The modern version believes the definition of subsistence level incorporates new technology. In effect, a higher minimum survival standard increases the average amount of raw materials necessary to assure the marginal person's survival. Instead of food and shelter, some people need gourmet food and designer clothes as a minimum. Children become status symbols rather than a labor intensive agricultural necessity. In reality, wealthier nations have lower birth rates. Malthus is proven wrong until technology inputs and the refined definition of survival meet.

Maslow's hierarchy of needs is usually expressed as a triangle with a broad base of physiological and safety needs. On an individual basis, basic survival requirements must be satisfied before further demands are considered. On a society-wide basis, the depression era zeitgeist best fits this description. After security, human desires turn to psychological needs - social acceptance. The first level is love, friends, other intimate relationships. On a societal scale, the zeitgeist of the 1960s best describes this level of evolution. The second level of psychological need involves wider social acceptance: accomplishment, esteem, and prestige. The 1980s symbolize this level of existence. Finally, the top of the pyramid describes self-actualizing goals: full potential and creative endeavors. When companies view social conscience as a form of profit, business moves into the self-fulfillment arena. Gestaltan is German for the smaller pieces serving as wholes, and many of these wholes create a large whole. Business models today reflect this gestalt, social profit, for example the company's green-ness, political correctness or employee welfare and life balance, may be more prestigious compared to financial profit. But, companies are expected to reflect these ethics in some way.

"The history of commerce is the history of civilization. In his barbarous state man's wants are few and simple, limited to his physical existence, such as food, clothing, and shelter, but as he advances in the scale of intelligence his wants increase and he requires not only the comforts and conveniences of life but even the luxuries." (Powers)

From Maslow's theory regarding the hierarchy of human needs to neo-Malthusian theories of survival strata to the words of O.M. Powers, the human determination to satisfy needs and then desires remains constant. The methods may change, the products may change, management approaches may change, but the survival instinct coupled with the taste for luxury does not change over time. Methods, products and management approaches change over time to reflect changing human desires. They are the response, not the stimulus.

Self-promotion and self-preservation are cornerstones to the consumer power structure of the Zero-Sum Cost marketplace. The long-term investment strategy imbedded in Zero-Sum Cost allows the consumer a hard times fund and a wealth creating fund, without a great deal of self-imposed frugality.

10 FRAMING THE QUESTION

How can society avoid Mellon's pain induced prudence?

Let's begin with this review   with Keynes as a cornerstone statement:

"All production is for the purpose of ultimately satisfying a consumer.

Time usually elapses , however - and sometimes much time – between the incurring of costs by the producer (with the consumer in view) and the purchase of the output by the ultimate consumer. Meanwhile the entrepreneur (including both the producer and the investor in this description) has to form the best expectations he can as to what the consumers will be prepared to pay when he is ready to supply them (directly or indirectly) after the lapse of what may be a lengthy period; and he has no choice but to be guided by these expectations, if he is to produce at all by processes which occupy time." (Keynes, 1964, 46)

Economists and heuristics agree the consumer ultimately controls outcome. Remember, Simon states solutions come from two methods: either choose from solutions or goods that already exists or innovation, create something unique. Regardless of which method is chosen, the success of the problem solver/decision maker rests in the hands of the consumer/end *user.* Entrepreneurs must estimate consumer desires over time and adjust accordingly. This reality implies the answer to the problem: eliminate the time lag by inviting the consumer into the process in the beginning. Von Hayek spoke of the damaging effects of the "pretence of knowledge" in his Nobel speech. The market is too difficult to predict. Why not eliminate, or at least, reduce that risk by allowing consumers to guide production choices?

Consider Nash and Simon: individuals want to conform in general but differentiate in specifics. Since knowledge isn't specific, especially predicting future trends, consumers will satisfice.

How can consumers and business partner in a free market economy to assure investment, savings, spending, employment, income and production all continue at sustainable growth rates? Technology. Remember, Solow's model found 80% of growth had its genesis in technology.

The consumer must integrate into the supply chain, and business profits by creating the infrastructure to do so.

Reviewing these facts and considerations, eliminating risk, and its associated costs, means engaging the consumer in the supply chain process early. The consumer considers their problem and seeks existing solutions, if none are found, they innovate, just like business.

Plugging this information and historical thoughts into the Keynes statement yields:

"All production is for the purpose of ultimately satisfying a consumer. The consumer/end user, if engaged early in the process, can eliminate risks and costs, and install guideposts leading to their satisficing. "

Consumer driven logistics becomes the obvious answer when the problem is framed properly. *This means that before a product can be designed, a project must be designed.* Risk reduction becomes the added value goal of this project.

11 DEFINITION / MOTIVATION FOR LOGISTICS

Commerce, including business, laws, technical developments, and even wars, is always subservient to the logic of the contemporary time and space. The final products and services have certainly changed greatly over time but the fundamental goal remains: to satisfy a need or a desire. Commerce today, as is it was in the very distant past, aims to satisfy the needs and wishes of an ever growing and sophisticated human population, including those of the businesses themselves.

Current business process trends show that one of the main stimuli of the twenty first century is planet-preservation. Similar to self-preservation in Maslow's hierarchy of needs, the planet stewardship ethic of a stakeholder affects the marketability of the end product with consumer preference supporting a fully integrated waste reduction program. Facing issues detailed in book titles such as: "Limits to Growth"[3] and "Silent Spring"[4] or in the different editorials from the more popular news outlets on global warming and the environment, it seems that planet earth is in such a dire position that it does not suffice to say that something is being done. More consumers demand the right processes must be carried out at the right time and at the right location in order for the world to sustain itself. This consumer ethic may be in its adolescence, but business leaders have already been influenced by this view.

"Logistics and supply chain management are not new ideas... It is only in the recent past that business organizations have come to recognize the impact that logistics management can have in the achievement of competitive advantage." (Christopher, 2005)

The internet revolution has not only shrunk the world, it has also increased the urgency for businesses to meet the needs and wishes of a global marketplace that is evolving at an accelerated pace. As the forces that drive change, particularly the "green revolution", matured during the last decade of the twentieth century and throughout the twenty-first century, businesses must evolve, adapt or close their doors. Under the pressure for greater efficiency, less transportation and less waste, businesses have started using the tools of supply chain management and logistics. Those two intertwined business activities aim to help companies survive the competitive and continuously changing nature of today's business environment.

"Logistics is the process of strategically managing the procurement, movement and storage of materials, parts and finished inventory (and the related information flows) through the organization and its marketing channels in such a way that current and future profitability are maximized through the cost-effective fulfillment of orders." (Christopher, 2005)

While this definition is not the unique and complete definition of logistics, it has the fundamental elements necessary for analysis. The fact that a business is trying to maximize its profit, current and future, is normal, but having to maximize a "social" profit through a lifecycle cost-effectiveness method is unprecedented. Perhaps the market system governance has evolved to a visible hand, where consumers insist on an entire supply chain advocacy of a green business ethic or some other social good. Adam Smith's invisible hand wielded immeasurable power, a power that can only be approximated by statisticians and actuaries. A more visible hand transfers the majority of that power to the consumer.

Consumers, using the Simon decision making

model, satisfice based on available goods and services or self-restraint in not consuming. In this way, traditionally, economic cost is transferred to consumers, those who are unable to negotiate the full terms of their transactions. Business simply competed with other suppliers of goods; they did not dissect the layers of consumer demand.

Environmental issues, for example, allowed businesses to engage in free services which cost consumers some lifestyle utility. Dumping waste, even heated water, into a river has been a standard in the past. Sophisticated consumers view these costs with a keener eye now. The modern sophisticated consumer views the products or services of a free rider polluter to not only cost in cash, but also in reduced societal lifestyle. Demand settles this issue in several ways: not in my back yard (NIMBY), there ain't no such thing as a free lunch (TANSTAAFL), and green economy.

Simply not allowing industrial plants to open nearby, or to demand the decommissioning of those that are open, or to regulate them out of business by increasing costs, does not answer the question: who's back yard do we pollute? The answer is find ways not to build free waste disposal into some businesses. But with this realization comes higher monetary costs of production. Placing consumers in this group of stakeholders deciding acceptable levels of tolerance helps the business budget for remediation and avoidance. Consumers will literally express the extent to which they will contribute to a cleaner environment. In some cases, the product line will terminate, asbestos insulation and brake pads, or lead paint for example. Energy providers have installed scrubbers and other smoke reducing technologies. Some jurisdictions limit automobile exhaust emissions. These environmental examples are all consumer driven.

The TANSTAAFL ethic, as it relates to this discussion, originated in the mid-1960s. Essentially, the ethic demands the social cost of environmental or other social issues arising out of profitable ventures should be funded from that profit. Emissions taxes, higher property taxes on blighted properties, and fuel taxes on trucks imply successful application. Developers who displace low income people to build luxury residences might be required to relocate the affected population into similarly affordable housing. Or, the local government may resolve these issues in order to charge luxury taxes on the new housing. But the social problem is addressed within the context of the project. As the consumer becomes more educated, more sophisticated, more activist, suppliers respond with socially responsive programs.

Certifications for green developments are an example of offering the sophisticated consumer some solace that their corporate partner is a good steward of the planet. Many modern companies insist on achieving an advanced level of certification for all facilities. Many companies are mindful of supply chain stakeholders' commitments to the social agenda. New developments require storm water management engineering to reduce excess runoff and the resultant erosion. More and more stakeholders consider consumer driven inputs for traditionally free downstream transfer of problems taboo. Solutions occur on site. It extrapolates logically then that consumers desire supply chain management to respond to this ethic.

With end users as stakeholders in the supply process, their input becomes readily available and more important. Buyers have always been undervalued as inputs. Environmentalism is not the only consumer driven ethic. Community service, decency in disaster relief, general positive citizenship and leadership, even positive role modeling services the consumers' needs to associate with favorable brands.

The main issue has always been maintaining a sufficient number of buyers. Consider Henry Ford creating his own buyers by inventing the assembly line. Historically, maybe the first attempt to literally have consumers involved in all production decisions and outputs. For proof we have the economic theories of supply and demand whose main objective, in very simple terms, is to balance the production side with the demand side. A business would be in good shape as long as it would try to keep cost on the low side. But as technology evolved over time and the market became more integrated, as the interests of the suppliers became confounded with that of the customers and consumers, a business would have to do more to stay profitable. Businesses were no longer able to count on and expect to have a certain number of customers or consumers solely based on past performance. Consumers would come and go in an instant and the business would be become very unpredictable. "A major contributing factor influencing the changed competitive environment has been the trend towards 'commoditization' in many markets".[6] Besides the many implications of a commodity market, such as no product differentiation or no customer loyalty, we think the important point here is that in a commodity market both consumers and producers would be directly negotiating their transaction which would mean that businesses and consumers hold equivalent stature. The full consequences of such equivalency are yet to be fully appreciated. The thing that is certain is that both businesses and consumers are faced with a fast changing environment.

The average consumer has risen to the self-actualization state in Maslow's hierarchy. The modern consumer concerns themselves with social issues along with selfish desires. Meanwhile, the marketplace is forever stuck in survival states of mind. The adaptation to more social awareness is symptomatic to survival skills in dealing with a more sophisticated consumer, not an actual transcendence of the profit motive.

12 DEFINITION / MOTIVATION FOR SUPPLY CHAIN MANAGEMENT

"Five major external forces seem to drive the rate of change and shape our economic and political landscape: globalization, technology, organizational consolidation, the empowered consumer, and government policy and regulation." (Coyle et al., 2008)

All of those factors are inter-related and each brings a specific set of requirements into the commercial process. Technology and the computer age spurred globalization. Globalization empowered consumers around the world. The empowered consumer and technology required organizational consolidation. Some notable firms foresaw this change coming and designed logistical supply chains with the future in mind.

With globalization, the commerce space is no longer limited by geo-political boundaries. In practice, attempts to regulate commerce politically only sends consumers to optional markets. The supply chain, and therefore consumerism, is politically free. The processes of procurement, of manufacturing, of storing, of transporting and of selling and marketing are non-uniform, non-linear, non-homogeneous, and non-continuous. It is almost as if commerce has evolved into a limitless and non-measurable activity. Any country attempting to regulate commerce damages its own economy.

With technology, commerce has greater control over the space and time of every transaction. The resources needed for a product can be artificially made, obtained overseas, or even brought in from outer space.

"Though the solar system's main asteroid belt is prohibitively far away, the near-earth region of outer space is chock-full of asteroids—tens of thousands at least 50 meters in diameter. Those asteroids, Planetary Resources co-founder Eric Anderson says, are lousy with platinum. Platinum is worth $1,500 an ounce.

The math isn't exact, but the potential value of the resource could be counted in the trillions of dollars."[9]

Technology has in many cases removed any limits to the resources and processes of businesses. However, as strictly a mining operation, the cost effectiveness of space mining for platinum is limited by the drop in value of the resource due to increased attainable abundance. Where technology resolves one issue, it tends to create another. In terms of business, technology has given greater access to consumers, and therefore, more control. End users have a greater symbiotic relationship with providers.

Technology and sciences mitigate the arguments in *Limits to Growth*. It is not only consumption that is growing exponentially but also new resources development and creation. With organizational consolidation, retailers have gained more control over the supply chain of many industries. Large retailers, such as Wal-Mart, control most of the aspects of production without acting as the actual producers. This organizational integration attains the goals of reducing the shelf price for the consumers without lowering standards of services, and at the same time reducing costs for the producers and the retailers.

Retailers are closest to their end consumers in the supply chain, and therefore, they are positioned to be more adept at creating values for those consumers. Retailers in many ways empower consumers who have yet to recognize their collective strength. Consumers are certainly being provided premium services in many respects, but they do not have the cost control that suppliers, wholesalers, manufacturers and retailers have in their respective industry. Yet, common sense and 200 years of economic thought agree consumers, or end users, ultimately control the profitability of the entire supply chain.

Call the process supply chain management, demand chain management, value network management, or logistics management; each process is primarily motivated by the concept that it is possible to maximize cost reduction by looking at commerce as a system. The concept of system analysis has worked well in many fields, and businesses seem to be doing a great job at implementing the process as "an extended enterprise that crosses the boundaries of individual firms to span the related activities of all the companies involved in the total supply chain. This extended enterprise should attempt to execute or implement a coordinated, two-way flow of good/services, information, and financials (especially cash)."[10]

Achieving these economies of scale means organizational consolidation. Supply chain management enhances this consolidation.

In this view of supply chain management, there are three important factors that show the motivation of business to be self-preservation and self-promotion. Self-preservation and self-promotion, which are basic to human needs (Maslow's safety and security, and esteem levels), will be achieved for profitable businesses if there are others around with whom to do business.

The first factor or principle of supply chain

management that we found relevant is reverse logistics. The idea that a business continues to be responsible long after a transaction has been completed speaks volumes in an environment with slogans such as buyer beware. Reverse logistics could even be seen as a source of cost control leading to profit for businesses. Instead of fighting after sales issues in the court, businesses find it better to save on time, lawyer fees and taxes. These advantages may even enhance the good image a business projects when it has a good reverse logistics in place.

Responsible business practices begin with honoring the spirit of the product or service. Good quality control reduces the frequency with which products are returned or payment for services refused. Quality assurance is the process of trading a defective product with a functioning product, or simply returning the money from the sale to the consumer. Quality assurance defines the reverse logistics element of business.

Business chooses between offering elite products and services or low end alternatives. Elite products feature guarantees and warrantees for serviceability and workmanship. Low end products may not. In either case, lawsuits do not enhance business reputations; and generally, they indicate a flawed business plans. The costs associated with not honoring returns exceed those of honoring them. Consumers communicate the risk they are willing to assume when they purchase high end products or service warrantees.

Business also chooses between honesty and deception. Consumers have united in this area by setting up reporting sites on the internet on which great, good, satisfactory, or poor service can be detailed. Business reputation can be a delicate dance with some consumers. This empowerment might be the first step in incorporating end users in the supply chain.

Information sharing is the second factor or principle of supply chain management found to be relevant. In a business world dominated by patent and trademark laws, the call for sharing information even among non-partners is unprecedented. The main reason for such information flow is that without it many large corporations would have failed. The larger a business gets the further away they get from the end-consumer. Large manufacturers need the small retailers to mine the information that will allow them to minimize cost. "If point-of-sale (POS) data were available from the retail level on a real-time basis, it would help to mitigate the bullwhip effect associated with supply chain inventories and could significantly reduce cost."[11]Sharing information helps companies stay competitive and relevant.

The purpose of patents and trademarks involves compensation for the inventor, owner, or author. Licensing these properties is the modern form of sharing technology while still maintaining the competitive edge. Consumers retreat from perceived greed. Sharing advances for a price is more polite.

Large manufacturers began distancing from end users prior to the computer revolution. The American automobile industry mired itself in large gas guzzlers prior to the gas crisis of the Carter Administration. Quicker to respond to consumer demand, the Japanese auto makers won a large market share, and have held it over time. The big three, Ford, General Motors and Chrysler lost touch with consumers.

The computer age allows manufacturers real time sales and returns data. Product sales reports include color preferences, sizes, retail price point information, virtually any data a manufacturer trying to control inventory costs might desire, and on an hourly basis.

The third and last factor or principle of supply chain management appears to be relevant is the need for financials management or cash flow management. Businesses do their best to minimize their cash outlay. Every company tries its best to minimize its cash-to-cash time. That is the time between investment and the return on the investment is reduced to its quickest. As a matter of fact, some companies manage to get paid first before they deliver any products or services. The case of Dell is a good example of such situation.

The just in time process perfected by Dell enables the company to get paid from the end consumer, get the assembled products from the suppliers before disbursing any capital. Actually Dell has the time to leverage the money that is due to its suppliers. Dell has no cost associated with inventory and is able to keep both its customers and its suppliers satisfied. This last factor of supply chain management combined with logistics is leading the way in creating a "Zero-Sum Cost" market place. It is already possible to say that most profitable companies are running without significant long-term economic cost. For those corporations any outlay of net cash is intended for generating maximum profit. Traditional cash depleting assets like inventory are minimized to just in time status. In that sense, any cash expenditure simply reflects the time value of money before profit accumulates. This cost structure exists throughout the supply chain until the consumer takes delivery of goods or services. Currently, the consumer never recuperates or passes through their costs.

13 DEFINITION / MOTIVATION FOR A ZERO-SUM COST®MARKET PLACE

Mathematical game theory concepts applied to business modeling and strategy originated with John von Neumann's proof of Brouwer's fixed point theorem in 1928. Continuous mappings into compact convex sets, better known as what if scenarios, became the standard method of game theory, and econometrics.

Von Neumann's paper was followed by his 1944 book Theory of Games and Economic Behavior, with Oskar Morgenstern, which considered cooperative games of several players. The second edition of this book provided an axiomatic theory of expected utility, which allowed mathematical statisticians and economists to treat decision-making under uncertainty. This foundational work contains the method for finding mutually consistent solutions for two-person zero-sum games.

Nash and Simon built on these theories. The zero-sum game theories, though, were dependent upon profit analysis and ignored the cost reduction process of business. In other words, game theory had evolved to a tactical tool and a behavioral prediction tool, but not a strategic tool.

During this time period, work on game theory was primarily focused on cooperative game theory, which analyzes optimal strategies for groups of individuals, presuming that they can enforce agreements between them about proper strategies."[12] While most of the literature refers to game theory as being applied to economics, it is easy to accept that any application to economics automatically leads to an application in the business world. Business and economics are closely related in that one provides the theoretical basis while the other is the experimental arena.

The zero-sum game concept , made popular by John Forbes Nash 's "EQUILIBRIUM POINTS IN N-PERSON GAMES"[13]combined with modern consumerism and technology implies successful implementation for a **Zero-Sum Cost®** market place. This theorem is commonly known as Nash Equilibrium.

"In game theory, Nash equilibrium (named after John Forbes

Nash, who proposed it) is a solution concept of a game involving two or more players, in which each player is assumed to know the equilibrium strategies of the other players, and no player has anything to gain by changing only his own strategy unilaterally. If each player has chosen a strategy and no player can benefit by changing his or her strategy while the other players keep theirs unchanged, then the current set of strategy choices and the corresponding payoffs constitute a Nash equilibrium."[14]

In this theorem and in much of game theory most of the attention is focused on maximizing the benefit, the gain, or the utility of all participants; or in the case of commerce, game theory optimizes the profits. The critics of Nash Equilibrium or of what is popularly known as zero-sum game have not failed to point out that this theory has very limited applicable use in day to day business activities.

"Due to the limited conditions in which NE can actually be observed, they are rarely treated as a guide to day-to-day behavior, or observed in practice in human negotiations.

However, as a theoretical concept in economics and evolutionary biology, the NE has explanatory power. The payoff in economics is utility (or sometimes money), and in evolutionary biology gene transmission, both are the fundamental bottom line of survival. "[14]

The problem with the analysis is the motivation behind zero-sum game theory is businesses or individuals are trying to maximize gain, profit and utility which are all intrinsically unbounded measures. Since Nash builds on classical economics, in competitive markets, economic profit always approaches zero. The difference between economic and financial profit confuses the analysts. Financial profit equals gross income less expenses. Opportunity costs, free rider costs, and other intangible costs are not included in the profit calculation. Economic profit includes these factors. Economic profit will be achieved in the short run by new industry pioneers and most monopolies or oligopolies; but for long-term competitive markets, economic profit hovers at zero, particularly in the aggregate.

Capital demands a return; an average return on investment is the opportunity cost referenced. With cycles of investment inflation, the capital sector reaps undeserved and riskless rewards. When the bust comes, those rewards are recaptured. Steady growth in investment leads to dynamic equilibrium in the markets. Pulsing money into the markets leads to the boom – bust cycle. For most consumers and investors, dynamic equilibrium increases lifestyle wealth better than perturbed markets.

The motivation for a **Zero-Sum Cost®** Market Place is focused on minimizing the cost for all participants of a business. The minimal cost has a lower bound of zero. It makes sense that the lowest cost one would pay for a product is zero and there should be no doubt that such position is achievable. Economically speaking, where there is no long-term achievable economic profit in competitive markets, economic costs are eliminated, actually transferred, as well. But this zero-sum speaks only to profit and loss, not to costs. Zero cost is not free. Zero cost means the economic costs are recuperated in the next transaction. The last payer in the last transaction is the consumer. So, in the current market place, the consumer never recuperates their costs.

14 HOW TO ACHIEVE A ZERO-SUM COST®MARKET PLACE

Any financially profitable business proves that it is possible to have a **Zero-Sum Cost®** Market Place. For those businesses, it is just a matter of time before any cost is translated into profit. Of course at any given time and for any particular product, it may difficult if not impossible to show a zero cost. Zero cost at any particular instant would mean free and the **Zero-Sum Cost®** Market Place is not promoting the business of giving or getting anything for free. The motivation for this method is similar to what drives the processes of business logistics and supply chain management: self-preservation and self-promotion. But this time a complete information set is envisioned where all parties involved: the suppliers, the manufacturers, the wholesalers, the retailers, the customers, are fully integrated as a system.

The only new element that is being proposed involves the cash-to-cash cycle also implemented for the end consumers as well as all the other participants of the market place.

The price a customer pays for any product includes different cost levels. Each of those costs is rightfully associated with some service level required by the customer. Extend that thought by implementing a system whereby one percent of the price of a product is put aside and invested in the market for the benefit of the consumer or end user. In fifty years with a rate of return of 9.75% compounded yearly, the consumer recovers his cost and more. "Berkshire's average annual rate of return over the last 20 years was 18.83%."[15] With 18.83% compounded annually would turn a one dollar ($1) investment into one hundred dollars ($100) in just about twenty seven years. A rate of return of 9.75% compounded annually would turn a one dollar ($1) investment into one hundred dollars ($100) in about fifty years. So it seems possible that one percent of price could guarantee a zero-sum cost over the appropriate length of time with the right and feasible rate of return from the market. Currently, cost recovery never occurs for the consumer.

15 RELATIONSHIP BETWEEN LOGISTICS, SUPPLY CHAIN MANAGEMENT AND THE ZERO-SUM COST® MARKET PLACE

Logistics and supply chain management represent a set of integrated processes used by businesses to minimize their financial cost without necessarily lowering quality in their products or services. In that regard, it should be understood that whatever cost that is left is transferred to the end consumer. Companies make profits by lowering the cost of their products for their consumers. One of the key processes of logistics and supply chain management is to compress the time in the cash-to-cash flow for businesses, suppliers, manufacturers and retailers. Extending the benefits of this process to the end consumers also would create the Zero-Sum Cost market place.

The cash-to-cash time for consumers would be compressed from never to fifty or even thirty years.

The precedent exists for companies to allow consumers to participate in a one percent cost rebate. Loyalty programs at grocery stores give gas discounts amounting to or exceeding one percent. Free flights on airlines can approach five or ten percent of the consumer cost structure. Pooling these rebates into an investment is technologically possible now. The economic benefits include savings and investments built into consumption.

16 THE SUCCESSES OF LOGISTICS AND SUPPLY CHAIN MANAGEMENT CREATE THE ENVIRONMENT FOR A DYNAMIC AND SUSTAINABLE ZERO-SUM COST® MARKET PLACE

As logistics and supply chain management become more successful for businesses, the business processes will become more integrated to the point where even the end consumers will be directly involve. There will be less volatility, less statistical estimation, because the communication channels going from suppliers passing through manufactures, retailers and the consumers would be visible and accessible to all parties. The concepts of total and complete information would become reality and would justify and support a **Zero-Sum Cost®** Market Place.

Keynes, von Hayek, Nash, Simon, and Solow all theorized how to achieve a "dynamic equilibrium" in the marketplace. A dynamic equilibrium minimizes fluctuations which, in turn, reduces major disturbances like recessions and depressions, booms and busts, bubbles and crashes. These great economists worked at a disadvantage, computer technology was not a factor in their proposals.

"Recessions, they claimed, were routine aspects of an economic cycle that must be endured, not cured." (Wapshott, 2011, 267) Classic economic theory separates consumers from producers, government intervention from citizen reaction, and investment from consumption while recognizing the impacts of these adverse effects of these codependent relationships.

Nash and Simon came close to the solution; zero-sum cost adds to their work by promoting a win – win scenario for consumers and producers alike. If consumption can include an element of savings and investment, if the consumer joins the supply chain and recovers costs, the market becomes so mutually dependent that misguided misallocations become detrimental to everybody, and the initiatives are never launched. The consumers and suppliers vote with their feet on an ongoing daily supply chain basis. This equation represents the breakeven point for consumers under the zero-sum cost market strategy.

Representing all transactions for all consumers

we have:

$$\sum_l \sum_m \left[P_{l,m} C_{l,m} (1 + I_{l,m})^{T_{l,m}} - C_{l,m} \right] = 0$$

$C_{l,m}$ is the cost to the consumer. In order for the consumer to recuperate their cost over time, an investment, a percentage of that cost, must be put in trust for the consumer's benefit. View that percentage like a loyalty program where in addition to ten cent discounts on gasoline, the consumer receives a donation to their retirement or investment fund.

$I_{l,m}$ is the rate of return on the investment contribution. I is obviously variable over time, but can be remarkably accurately predicted over long periods of time. The key variable is the time required to reduce the consumer cost to zero. Under current policy, this event never occurs.

Time is expressed as years (T). The bottom line meaning behind this equation is that some percentage of the cost of a good, if invested at an average rate of return for a period of time, some if not all of the costs borne by the consumer will be returned as an investment as the economy grows. The investment in the economy as a percentage of consumption, according to all the economists, will help grow the economy indefinitely.

For the purposes of this analysis, one percent will be used as the universal contribution. In a competitive market, the consumer may demand a greater percentage and this may be a supplier point of competition. With end users fully integrated into the decision process of the supply chain, this discussion of residual re-investment becomes natural, even inevitable. The formula simplifies to:

$.01(1 + I)^T = 1$

when one percent is substituted and both sides of the equation are divided by the actual cost. The true variables become the interest rate or return on investment (I), and the time in years (T). Since consumers become lenders and investors, businesses have an incentive to treat consumers ethically and fairly. Since consumers are investors, consumers have an incentive to make the businesses successful. Excellent feedback cycles are built into this arrangement. Financial cost cutting and thrift flow naturally from this system.

The strength of this plan is that no matter what the return on investment is and no matter how much time is required at that rate to recover costs, the timeframe is shorter than never, the current strategy. At ten percent return, the average on the stock market for the long-term, the consumer recovers costs in 50 years. Consumers will literally be invested in suppliers, businesses, savings, economic profit, economic costs, supply and demand, and by extension, government spending and taxes. Consumption brings an element of investment. A consumers' retirement fund built into the commerce system.

Nearly every investment strategy for small investors relies on early deposits and compound interest. The magic of compound interest is sold in IRAs, dollar cost average investing, or simple savings accounts. The principal is sound. The earliest dollar invested will double in value more times than late investment.

Consider a real estate transaction. Real estate brokers receive a commission based on points. Mortgage lenders fees are generally one or two percent. If the buyer were to bank one percent also, the real estate investment would become diversified. The buyer could recuperate costs through the zero-sum cost plan, and the home would strictly serve as a hedge against housing inflation. Homeowners, as part of the supply chain, would shun subprime mortgage markets as destructive. Tax payers do not have that power or luxury, equity owners do.

Now consider a product that has failed in the marketplace. It is antiquated or replaced by a newer version, but the manufacturer still has inventory, an unrecovered cost. In a consumer driven, better knowledge supply chain, these products could recover the cost more efficiently since a "Dutch auction" would naturally occur. The asking price is lowered until it meets the best bid. That bid will take a number of units out of circulation and recover some costs for the manufacturer. The next highest bid will do the same, only less cost recovery for the manufacturer. And so on until the product is sold out and discontinued. Even losses are minimized; but they can be avoided with just in time inventories driven by consumer inputs.

Recall the earlier question, "How can consumers and the business sector partner in a free market economy to assure investment, savings, spending, employment, income and production all continue at sustainable growth rates?"

Compare to traditional discount programs Zero-Sum Cost® not only promotes spending but it helps build savings and investment. This essentially means that consumers (individuals, families or business) are directly participating in the investment market, under similar conditions and mutual policing. If incorporated into all consumption, housing, food, transportation, major appliances, furniture, even the morning coffee, consumers and suppliers begin to understand the mutually beneficial relationship everybody's hard work and superior service provide. Investment leads to employment opportunity. Full employment leads to increased wage rates. Full employment at higher wages leads to greater investment. The economy continually grows at a stable rate.

With new technologies like Dwolla, virtual wallets, paypal and other on line banking and investment facilities, zero-sum costing can be used in any transaction with the consumer dividend paid directly to their investment account. Some grocery store in house banks, and bank owned credit cards, have implemented this strategy by rounding up purchases to the nearest dollar or ten dollars and automatically depositing the difference into the consumer's savings account. This service has not gained a great deal of traction because the consumer is simply transferring money from one account to another, and then when the bill comes due, they transfer back to checking and pay it. The savings gain is zero.

Think about the credit card surcharge or the cash discount debate discussed in terms of Simon's bounded rationality. Whether cash payments receive a discount or credit card purchases are charged a servicing fee, the difference is strictly nuanced. But the wording affected buying habits. People want conformity and belonging. The sense that paying cash is normal or the exception became an important distinction. In zero-sum costing, gross points are considered a bonus, just like that ten cent discount on gasoline.

The consumer knows they're paying for the gasoline discount, but it feels like a perquisite. In a fully integrated supply chain, the consumer understands the costs are passed to the consumer, but the savings and investment perquisite attaches the consumer directly to the supply chain business. It feels like a bonus. It will be treated as a bonus savings and investment plan, strictly long-term.

17 HOW CAN BUSINESS EVOLVE IN THIS PARADIGM

Evolution requires change. This can be scary, but it's natural. Some business decisions seem so insignificant, like whether or not to renew a magazine subscription, hardly worth the time to consider. This attitude is a mistake with zero-sum cost marketing. Consumers will look for waste and unnecessary spending when choosing a consumption partner. Business will be lean when all stakeholders have access to the intimacies of the business.

Modern marketing techniques do at least two things well: they attract the profitable customer, the target market is better defined, and they announce arrival into the twenty-first century loudly.

The old real estate adage: location, location,

location has been replaced with: access, access, access. Cyberspace is unlimited in size and cheap rent, but most important: highly accessible. Domino's demonstrated explosive growth based on expanding customer access. If a customer had a phone, Domino delivered a hot pizza in one-half hour. In the modern business model, physical location is relatively unimportant as long as accessibility is built into the model.

If a modern consumer were shopping for a new car, they would not google "horseless carriages". Of course not! The fact that they are googling anything means the modern consumer has changed their shopping habits. Businesses must speak the language of the consumer and in the format the consumer chooses. Young and elderly alike use the internet to research goods and services. This technology is completely integrated into the marketplace. If a business hasn't changed advertising media, what message are they sending potential customers? "We're old school", that's the message. Modern consumers will not spend time anticipating antiquated goods.

Today, there are more ways to compare businesses and the goods and services they provide. The customers are more sophisticated. So in order to survive and thrive, business must evolve. Business entities must stop being nostalgic about past marketing strategies. Has anyone ever replaced an old jacket from high school because the collar is frayed? No, consumers do not spend money on false memories.

A business will not replace an assembly line with the same machinery originally purchased thirty years ago. Newer equipment is better, more energy efficient, more productive, and as a result, more competitive. In the computer age, old school phone book advertising seems silly. Unless a company has time to give lowball, no profit bids to penny pinching customers whose time is best spent calling every business trying to save a dollar on a set of tires, the business targets its marketing to preferred consumers. Worst of all, it costs serious money to use traditional print media. This decision is toxic in a leaner supply chain economy. Business cannot use yesterday's media to attract tomorrow's customer.

The big companies know that first impression is critical. The CEO's wife doesn't cobble together a flyer to stick under windshields. Unfortunately, the information is lost because the presentation is so poor. For that state-of-the-art tire store, the flyer or phone book ad yells amateur, shade tree mechanic. Business must evolve to be a twenty-first century business, and this means throughout the supply chain including the customer.

Artwork, logos, and pictures generate emotions more readily than "match any offer" ever will. The current young professionals were raised on fancy electronic games, not flashlight tag. They need stimulation and all their senses engaged. People buy emotionally. Modern business image includes the entire big world-wide picture. The consumer wants to experience that from inside the business. Zero-sum cost marketing accomplishes this feat.

Fire the worst clients, or better yet, do not acquire them. The excessive complainers, rude and hostile people, excessive returners, the know-it-all ignoramus, the call-all-hours-at-homes, the something-for-nothings, the mission creepers, the competitor-does-this-for-less, the 20% that causes 80% of the problems yet provides none of the profit create costs which can never be recovered in modern business. Screen the customers and do not get trapped into allowing them to be repeat customers. They are toxic to good customers. Zero-sum cost marketing basic logic implies collaboration. Customers give honest and specific information up front as to their needs and desires that will *satisfice* their requirements. No hidden agendas, no costs spiraling out of control. And the best part: the customer has a stake in the final outcome. The customer receives goods and services and an Investment to reduce their costs.

Word of mouth advertising and marketing will always be cost effective and welcome by business. Consider each transaction an opportunity to partner a need with a solution. Zero-sum cost marketing extends this ethic to helping the customer recover costs. The internet has already taken word of mouth to the next level with chat rooms and consumer reporting pages.

Almost every good can be sold via the internet. Customers all over the world can access a local, small town store at any time and buy goods, as long as the store is visible and accessible. Most services can be sold online. The immediate gratification epidemic drives this multitasking "resolve all issues now" mentality of net surfing. If customers cannot access company information, a willing and technically savvy competitor is one click away. Even location oriented businesses, such as gasoline retailers, need to compete on price over a wider geographic area since websites exist to list local gasoline prices. Grocery chains install pumps and run loyalty specials on gasoline. Again, access, not location. Convenience is a strong emotional buying condition, people buy emotionally.

Modern competitive businesses need to know who is their customer, even if the customer has never been seen at a location. The days of knowing the good customers by sight are numbered for most product retailers. However, data mining for target customers is a growth industry. In zero-sum cost marketing strategies, the customer becomes part of the team. Pick the ones you want on the team. Personal data about where customers live, work, birth dates, husbands, wives, boyfriends' and girlfriends' birth dates, names of children, habits and hobbies, and, of course, phones and email addresses, can be mined for similarities or used for special contacts. Individual and collective customer buying habits (the when, what, why, where and how information) point to inventory needs, specials to run, targets to present.

This information gathering and data analysis is simple through technology. The ensuing communications allow the business to become part of a family or another business. The idea of presenting an investment as part of consumerism reinforces this communal feel.

In the insurance business, agents send birthday cards to their clients' spouse. To sell more insurance? No. To remind their client the birthday is coming up, and to receive the endorsement of the spouse. There are a million reasons to gather this information and another million uses. Use the data wisely to create a client from a customer, provide targeted timely information, or to better the personal relationship in an increasingly impersonal world. Another card they send is for the customer's life insurance birthday, six months after the actual birth date. Why? Because life insurance age changes on that day, and additional premiums would rise unless the client bought more insurance before that date. The agent employs the marketing strategy of explaining a cost increase soon, motivating the client to act now. Any business can employ this strategy. How about a vet or a pet store sending out six dog birthday greetings a year to dog owners, suggesting chew toys, tick and flea medications, leashes, or any overstocked item? Emotionally, clients respond well to thoughtful and timely offers, not well to nudging. With this in mind, businesses which communicate investment bonuses to loyal partners in their supply chain will be received well, and the data received from that partnership will help increase profits.

If the internet and ecommerce has succeeded in any way, getting paid for goods and services is it. Customer convenience, flexible payment options, and immediate collection and deposit earmark ecommerce. Besides checks and credit cards, the internet banking-payment-receivable services include PayPal and its ilk, ebay and other auction sites, amazon.com and other mass consignment sites. These services allow clients every convenience in paying.

The zero-sum cost market strategy enables the consumer investment account to be paid just as easily. Cash to cash times drop to minimums through cyberspace.

New marketing replaces old school scattershot, "please come to us" marketing with "we'll come to you" approaches. Target potential clients, find them, be more profitable. New marketing is as much about lifestyle, convenience and happiness as it is about profit.

Successful zero-sum cost marketing businesses incorporate these ethics with the investment sharing strategy of cost recovery. The innovation of adding the end user to the supply chain as a partner in commerce creates an information flow in both directions which enables better, more cost effective supply chain inventory management and cost recovery strategies. Marketing to loyal customers becomes integral to that process.

The end user has responsibility in this paradigm. Consumers will need to determine what costs are associated with specific suppliers and what costs are acceptable.

The consumer, of course, chooses the specific product from a variety of suppliers. The consumer is choosing a supply chain at the same time. Consumers can demand, or at least vote, on a code of ethics, general business practices, community involvement, political and social cause support, simple low cost, or environmental stewardship. The consumer chooses the most satisficing bundle of goods reflecting their values.

Modern businesses brand strategy includes more social conscience than in the past. When consumers become intimate with the supply chain, demands will rise in this arena. Ethics will be measured carefully and continuously on the internet. Consumers have begun this process already. Social networks spread concerns and Kudos quickly.

General business practices will also be scrutinized. Fairness in dealings, employee satisfaction, minimum wages, even in foreign markets, general employee welfare are all potential issues on which consumers view as relevant. One issue might be the difference between CEO compensation and the average employee wage. Consumers may view outrageously large salaries or perquisites to be cost sucking extras to be reduced or eliminated. Consumer pressure, especially investment and supply chain partners can bring some pressure to change the more egregious practices.

Modern consumers support business that is community minded. Ben and Jerry successfully joined community and business through ice cream. The response proved tremendous. Perhaps homebuilders will be expected to donate labor downtime or extra materials to Habitat for Humanity or similar operation. Grocery stores may change waste reduction strategies to feed the homeless rather than sell deeply discounted food just before expiration. The consumer partner will communicate through supporting business that share their ethic.

Low cost will always survive. Low cost suppliers will attract the customers who just want a commodity for a price. No special citizenship requirements.

Environmental stewardship has already created adjustments in how supply chains work. Xerox created one of the first completely recycle-able machines in the computer industry. Ink cartridges were designed to be refilled, all plastic was made from recycled materials to be recycled. The market responded very positively to this design.

Consumers live in communities affected by blight and pollution. They prefer risk avoidance to remediation.

The zero-sum cost market strategy, through its openness, has a risk management aspect built in. Business cannot afford to sell defective supplies or their entire supply chain, and their alternative supply chain, knows immediately about the problem. The absence of secrets creates more trust.

The process will be iterative. The Persuasion and Evocation model from Simon is a best fit process for decision making. The system processes premises or assumptions (inputs), and draws conclusions (outputs). Company goods and services are offered as solutions to needs. These either work as promised or they do not. Either output leaves only certain options; and creates the next input. This conclusion serves as the next input, or educated assumption. The persuasion cycle responds only to the selected premises, therefore, the assumption or premise shape the potential solutions or output.

Unfortunately, conflicting inputs are not rare. In business, time, competition, consumer demands, raw materials and technological changes can affect available inputs. Consumers will need to demand a value proposition rather than an end result with a business code of ethics to encompass all the social and environmental desires of the stakeholders.

Business becomes project oriented rather than product oriented.

Originally, this type of research questioned the motivation of individuals or special interest groups to participate in inputs. Since inputs steer a decision toward a desired goal, a corporate goal, or in the belief that the goal is in the best interest of the community, inputs had to be questioned, vetted. In this communal process, conflicting inputs are actually welcomed. The most satisficing result expects some conflict. Once institutional structures that traditionally block innovation reduce in influence, ideology and self-interest are secondary hurdles.

18 SOME INDUSTRIES WHICH COULD INCORPORATE ZSC SEAMLESSLY

Two obvious industries which could begin implementing this marketing strategy are Health and human services providers and the finance and insurance industries. This marketing strategy is a natural extension of their products and services. The hotel/restaurant/hospitality industry has many loyalty programs and this 1% added technique would fit in to the long-term use of retirement money. The science and technology sector can benefit from ZSC immediately.

Innovations like the health savings plans have already paved the way for long-term savings funds. More importantly, demand is inelastic for health services. People will pay more to get the service at any supply level. Industry wide gross profit averages 90.63% with an average SGA (Sales, general and administrative expense) of 25.37. Surely the consumer can reduce costs with feedback on services to save 1%. This money can be put in trust for long-term care or illnesses.

The finance and insurance industries already have the infrastructure in place for this type of product. With a 99.83% gross profit, the sale is essentially trust driven, the product is increasing the client's money. The SGA averages 24.49 in this industry and benefits/retirement funding is 50% greater than other industries. Certainly 1% can be squeezed out for the customer, especially in a wealth building industry.

The restaurant, hotel, and hospitality industry averages a gross profit of 61% with an SGA of 16.76%. The strategy in this industry involves financing future end users. Older people tend to spend their savings on more luxury goods and travel. They seek feedback from customers constantly. Why not include them in the business strategy?

The science and technology sector has a gross profit of 73.28% and an SGA of 18.95. Technology is driven by consumer convenience and innovation. Consumers and end users must be part of this supply chain in order to keep this industry lively. And, the money is there to do so. Also, the entire ZSC market strategy requires updated consumer technology in order to function effortlessly.

Any long-term investment goods or services should begin now because the early investments will be worth the most in the future. This approach stabilizes these markets for years.

19 **CONCLUSION**

The big picture regards the stabilizing effect the zero-sum costing approach brings to the overall economy.

$$\sum_{l} \sum_{m} \left[P_{l,m} C_{l,m} (1 + I_{l,m})^{T_{l,m}} - C_{l,m} \right] = 0$$

Each consumer choice involves allocating assets, directly and irreversibly. The end user will demand a percentage of the overall costs to produce. For example, highly competitive commodity products, like laundry detergent or toilet paper, may try to differentiate through qualitative selling, premium product claims, or quantitative methods like price or zero-sum costing percentages. In this way, consumer taste for investments will allocate resources to the correct supplier. Investment and savings choices are made when consumption decisions are made. The balance in the economy becomes natural. The consumer says premium soap is worth one point of investment, or for two points, the laundry can be slightly less clean. Old inventories are replaced with new consumer designed, or at least consumer inspired, inventories created by new technologies supported by the consumers own investment. This investment ultimately recovers the consumer's costs associated with brand loyalty.

The balance between investment and consumption, particularly for lower and middle class families, is better reflected in the zero-sum costing paradigm. The lower and middle class consumer must spend most of their incomes on survival needs. Asset allocation means survival first, luxury second. The suppliers might respond to this reality by offering low cost food and shelter price points without an investment premium. On the other hand, suppliers may market to this level by offering a retirement plan like the big bosses get for just a few pennies more.

Specialty savings or investments are possible. Companies catering to baby products could offer college fund savings. Vitamin companies or even family pharmacies could offer a medical savings account. Residential real estate companies might offer assisted living savings or investments. Younger buyers begin funding distant future needs.

All of these scenarios can be negotiated through

the logistics and supply chain management system whereby consumers have access to the early decisions in products and services.

Keynes would appreciate the built in investment and savings strategy that did not rely on individual thrift. The demand side strategy of allowing end users to be stakeholders in design and distribution of goods and services would appeal to him.

Von Hayek would applaud the system's reduction in monetary stimulus through built in technological investment. Each component of the system relies on the others for cash to cash motion. The flow is truly circular rather than linear.

Of course, the zero-sum cost market is based on the works of Nash and Simon.

Solow would approve of the built in technology investments to create growth.

Remember, investments in new technology spur 80% of all the growth in the economy. The zero-sum cost market uses the profits from current technology to fund future technologies through a consistent investment program designed for long-term growth. Business people study return on investments as a success measurement. If the zero-sum cost marketplace strategy reduces company costs by 2% through more efficient and timely communications with customers, and the business splits this savings with the customer, the US economy frees over 200 billion dollars to be invested in new technologies, the driving force behind growth. All boats rise with this tide.

In five years, one trillion dollars re-enters the investment markets as consumer participation. If that one percent investment strategy returns an average stock market return plus a dividend for the influx of new technology created, in fifty years the consumer investment asset conservatively grows to 15 trillion dollars.

This proposed partnership raises the living conditions of everyone and assures economic growth for the long run. "Livability is not a middle-class luxury. It is an economic imperative." - Robert Solow

REFERENCES

Augier, Mie and Frank, Katherine Simon. (2002) "Introduction: Herbert A. Simon (1916-2001)".

Industrial and Corporate Change, 11:3. (583-86)

Batra, Ravi. (2005) *Greenspan's fraud: How two decades of his policies have undermined the*

global economy. New York: Palgrave Macmillan.

Bhaskaran, Anand; Parihar, Rahul & Prakhya, Srinivas. (2008) "Approaches to Decision Making

Under Uncertainty". *IIMB Management Review.* June, 2008. (228-239)

Black, William K. (2005). *The best way to rob a bank is to own one: How corporate executives*

and politicians looted the S&L industry. Austin, Texas: University of Texas Press.

Cyert, Richard M. (1979) "Portrait: Herbert

Simon". *Challenge.* (Sep-Oct) (62-4)

Federal Reserve Statistical Release. (2011, March 3) *Money Stock Measures.* Web.

Friedman, Milton. (1994) *Money mischief: Episodes in monetary history.* New York, USA:

Harcourt Brace & Company.

Gidel, T., Gautier, R. & DuChamp, R. (2005) "Decision-making framework methodology: an

original approach to project risk management in new product design". *Journal of Engineering Design.* 16:1 (1-23)

Hunt, Norman C. (1980) "Herbert Simon: appreciation and aspiration". *Managerial and*

Decision Economics, 1:1. (1-3)

Hutchuel, Armand. (2001) "Towards Design Theory and Expandable Rationality: the unfinished

program of Herbert Simon". *Roundtable: Cognition, Rationality and Governance*.

(260-273)

Keynes, John Maynard. (1964) *The General Theory of employment, interest, and money.* New York, USA: Harcourt Brace & World, Inc.

Lyon, Herbert L. and Simon, Julian L. (2001) "Price elasticity of the Demand for Cigarettes in

the United States". *American Journal of Agricultural Economics* (888-895)

Mankelwicz, John and Kitahara, Robert. (2010) "Quantification, Rationality, and Management

Decisions". *Journal of Business & Economics Research,* 8:5 (59-70)

Mayer, Martin. (2001) *The Fed: The inside story of how the world's most powerful financial*

institution drives the markets. New York: The Free Press.

Mockler, Robert J. (1968) "The Systems Approach to Business Organization and Decision

Making". *California Management Review.* 11:2 (53-58)

Mousavi, Shabnam and Garrison, Jim. (2003) "Toward a transactional theory of decision

making: creative rationality as functional coordination in context." *Journal of Economic*

Methodology. 10:2 (131-156)

NetMBA. (2011) "PERT". *NetMBA: Business Knowledge Center.*

http://netmba.com/operations/project/pert/. Web. Accessed 19 March 2011.

Roche, Cullen. (2011) *The myth of the exploding U.S. money supply*. Pragmatic Capitalism-Blog.

Retrieved March 7, 2011, from Seeking Alpha Web site: http://seekingalpha.com/article/256913-on-the-myth-of-exploding-u-s-money-supply

Saunders, Anthony and Cornett, Marcia Millon. (2007) *Financial markets and institutions: An*

introduction to the risk management approach. New York: The McGraw-Hill Companies, Inc.

Sent, Esther-Mirjam. (2005) "Simplifying Herbert Simon". *History of Political Economy* 37:2.

(227-232)

Simon, Herbert A. etal. (1987) "Decision Making and Problem Solving". *Interfaces,* 17:5. (11-31)

Simon, Herbert A. (2001) "Administrative Decision Making". *Public Administration Review.*

(31-7)

Wapshott, Nicholas. (2011) *Keynes Hayek: The Clash That Defined Modern Economics*. New York, USA: W. W. Norton & Company.

Wells, Donald R. (2004) *The Federal Reserve System: A history*. Jefferson, North Carolina:

McFarland & Company, Inc.

http://www.tradingeconomics.com/Economics/Unemployment-Rate.aspx?Symbol=USD

Footnote sources:

1. Commerce and Finance, O. M. Powers

2. Logistics and Supply Chain Management Creating Value-Adding Networks, Martin Christopher

3. Limits to Growth, Donella Meadows, Jorgen

Randers, and Dennis Meadows

4. <u>Silent Spring</u>, Rachel Carson

5. <u>Logistics and Supply Chain Management Creating Value-Adding Networks,</u> Martin Christopher

6. <u>Logistics and Supply Chain Management Creating Value-Adding Networks,</u> Martin Christopher

7. <u>Logistics and Supply Chain Management Creating Value-Adding Networks,</u> Martin Christopher

8. <u>Supply chain Management A Logistics Perspective</u> , Coyle, Langley, Gibson, Novack, Bardi

9. http://www.slate.com/articles/technology/future_tense/2012/05/asteroid_mining_the_crazy_awesome_plan_to_grab_platinum_f rom_outer_space_.html , 5/16/2012 4:17AM

10. <u>Supply chain Management A Logistics Perspective</u> , Coyle, Langley, Gibson, Novack, Bardi

11. <u>Supply chain Management A Logistics Perspective</u> , Coyle, Langley, Gibson, Novack, Bardi

12. http://en.wikipedia.org/wiki/Game_theory , 5/19/12 7:51 am

13. MATHEMATICS: J. F. NASH, JR. Vol., 36 1950 page 48-49

14. http://en.wikipedia.org/wiki/Nash_theorem _(in_game_theory), 5/19/12 9:56 am

15. http://allfinancialmatters.com/2008/04/02/ a-look-at-berkshire-hathaways-annual-market-returns-from-1968-2007/ 5/19/12 2:55pm

Index

acceptance 37
accounts   16
achievable 64
Achieving 23
administrative   27
alternatives   27
analysis   28
annually   66
anything   12
application   61
approach   30
approaches 38
assumption 29, 86
assurance 56
asteroids 53
averages   88
birthday   82
business   43-47, 50, 55-57, 61, 65, 74,
77-80, 82, 84-86, 92
businesses 45, 47, 50, 55-56, 67, 72,
78, 81, 83
changing   62
checking   16
choosing   25
collapses 8
commerce   44, 53
commodity 50
communications   24
community 85
companies 13, 91
competitive   63
completion 31
components 24
compound   73
compounded 66
computer   58
concerns   2

condition 26
conditions 32
conformity 29
Confrontation 32
Consider   49, 73
consolidation 52, 55
constraints   22
construction   30
consumer   1-2, 5, 14, 17-18, 33, 40-43,
45, 47-50, 52, 59, 64, 66, 71, 75, 78,
80, 84-85, 88, 90-91, 93
consumers   4-6, 18, 33, 41-42, 46-47,
49-50, 54, 57-58, 67-70, 72, 74, 78,
84-86
consumption   70
contribution   19, 71
convenience   83
corporate   2
currency   7, 16
customer   66, 78-82
customers   50, 78, 80-81
decision   21-28, 33
decisions   21-23, 25-26, 28
definition 37, 46
deliberation   33
deposits   16
depression 10-11, 13
describes   37
designed   30, 43
difference 75
differences   32
directly   75
discount   75
distinctive   3
ecommerce   83
economic   3, 11, 22, 63-64, 70, 72, 93
economics   11, 61-62
efficiency 35
eliminate   41-42

Emissions 48
employee 84
employment 12, 74
empowered 52
enterprise 55
Entrepreneurship 13
environment 50
environmental 48
equilibrium 18, 61-63, 70
evolutionary 62
excessive 80
expectations 14
extended 55
feedback 88
financial 4, 8, 63
Friedman 9
function 4
gasoline 75, 81
globalization 52
government 4, 7, 9-13
Hamilton 8
honoring 56
Hutchuel 25
important 34
incentive 72
includes 16
including 44
individuals 19-20
industries 87-88
industry 88
inflation 17
information 22, 57, 82
innovation 25, 29-30, 33
insolvent 17
institutions 8
insurance 17, 82
interest 29, 73
Interestingly 13
internet 6, 83

inventories   91
inventory 59
investment 4, 16-17, 58, 63, 66, 70-75, 83, 91-93
investments   4, 13, 91-92
investors 72
knowledge 41-42
language   31
lifestyle 47
location   77-78, 81
logistics 45-46, 56, 67, 69
long-term 87
lowering   67
maintained 11
management 27-28, 30-32, 38, 45, 49, 55, 58, 67, 69
managerial 21
managers   23
Mankelwicz 23
manufacturer   74
manufacturers 58
marketing 5, 15, 77, 80, 83, 87
marketplace   1
materials 34, 85
mathematical   28, 60
maximize   5, 46
merchant   5
minimize   58
mortgage   73
motivation 36, 63
observations   21
observed   62
offering   91
Operational   28
opportunity   63
optimization   24
organizational   52, 54
oriented   33
particular 65

```
percentage 71
performance    30
perquisite 75
persuasion 86
planning   11
platinum   53
politically    53
population 36
positive   49
practices 84
predicted 13
premises   86
pressure   85
prisoners 26
processes  28,  31,  53,  67
producer   14,  40
producers 54,  70
production 41-42,  49
products   38,  56,  67
projects   12,  32
psychological 37
purchases 75
quantification    23
quantitative  25
rational   23
rationality    21-23
received   83
recessions 70
recycled   85
reducing   54
regulate   53
relevant   57
Remember   41-42
replaced   78
resolution 27
resources  34,  53
Responsible    56
retailers 54,  81
revolution 36,  45
```

satisficing   24
scenarios 28
self-preservation 55
self-promotion   55
services   2, 4, 47, 54, 56, 78, 83, 87, 92
shopping 78
solutions 23, 25, 27, 41-42, 86
something 25
sophisticated 47-48
specific   84
spending   10-11, 74
stakeholders 31, 49
statement 12
stimulus   13
strategies 61
strategy   15, 19-20, 62, 82-83, 87-88, 92
suggests   20
Summarized 11
suppliers 33, 59, 84, 91
survival   37-38, 50, 91
technology 3-4, 17, 34, 37, 41-42, 52-54, 88, 92
theories   61
therefore 23, 54
transaction   64
trillion   93
ultimately 14
understanding 32
unemployment 10, 13
unquantifiable   22
variable   71
wholesaler 5
zeitgeist 37
zero-sum   1, 14-15, 19, 33, 61, 63, 65, 67, 69-70, 75, 80, 83, 90, 92

www.ingramcontent.com/pod-product-compliance
Lightning Source LLC
Chambersburg PA
CBHW060622210326
41520CB00010B/1434